HOW·TO
WRITE
TO WORLD
LEADERS

HOW·TO

WRITE

TO WORLD
LEADERS

RICK LAWLER

AVON BOOKS ◆ NEW YORK

AVON BOOKS
A division of
The Hearst Corporation
1350 Avenue of the Americas
New York, New York 10019

Library of Congress Cataloging in Publication Data:
Lawler, Rick, 1949–
    How to write to world leaders / by Rick Lawler.—1st ed.
        p.   cm.
Includes bibliographical references
1. Heads of state—Directories.   2. Letter-writing—Handbooks, manuals, etc.   I. Title
JF37.L38   1990
351.003'025—dc20   89-27317
                                                                  CIP

First Avon Books Printing: January 1992

AVON TRADEMARK REG. U.S. PAT. OFF. AND IN OTHER COUNTRIES, MARCA REGISTRADA, HECHO EN U.S.A.

Printed in the U.S.A.

OPM 10 9 8 7 6 5 4 3 2 1

Dedicated to, of course, Tang Yih-Ying
and
Sara Melissa Lawler

A special thanks must be made to embassy employees who so kindly provided information and checked the accuracy of their respective nation's listing.

Disclaimer

Considering the troubles Salman Rushdie has had from Islamic nations with the publication of his book *Satanic Verses*, I feel it's necessary to include a disclaimer.

The possibility, however slight, exists that you could get yourself into trouble when communicating with the leaders of foreign nations. The written word has the power to anger as well as appease, whether those words appear in a book or in a letter.

Therefore you need to be aware of this:

How to Write to World Leaders, its authors, editors, publishers, printers, researchers, those distributing it, retail outlets, and libraries will *not* be responsible for any trouble you get yourself into using the information in this book.

You are solely responsible for your own actions and the results of those actions. If you write the Libyans and get them mad at you, for example, you're on your own.

While we have made every effort to confirm the accuracy of the information in this book, we are not responsible for errors or omissions.

Contents

Foreword

When I first examined a preliminary version of this book, it struck me as an odd idea. Why a book listing names and addresses of world leaders? To whom was this book directed? What was its target audience?

This is, after all, quite a thin volume. It is not loaded down with facts and figures, essays, and many of the other things that add to the bulk of annual directories and resource tomes.

How to Write to World Leaders, after much reflection, may turn out to be one of the more useful books published in recent years—for a number of very good, practical reasons.

To whom is this book directed? I've given it quite some thought, and have developed a long list (certain that you may add to it). I share part of this list below:

- Politicians
- Government employees engaged in foreign affairs
- Business people involved in foreign trade and commerce.
- Organizations and associations that support or oppose various causes, including environmental, human rights, political, ethnic, nationalistic, and many others.
- Public libraries, of course.
- College, university, high school and elementary school libraries.
- Teachers

- Journalists and writers.
- Religious organizations.
- Professors and students of political science, international relations and other university departments.
- Everyday citizens like you and me, who have an interest in world affairs and sometimes a desire to make our opinions and ideas known to leaders of countries other than our own.

As you can readily see, the list is a long one (and by no means complete).

This book, I imagine, may create its own market as people become aware of its existence *and what can be done with it*, giving everyone who desires a voice in world affairs.

I can't imagine why someone has not thought of such a book before. It is, quite simply, a marvelous idea. Perhaps we have not written world leaders to any great extent simply because it never occurred to us to do so. Perhaps by having the names and addresses at hand, more and more citizens of one nation will express their opinions to leaders of other nations.

What the final result of this new idea may be, I cannot begin to imagine.

Today, with this book, it's infinitely easier for individuals and groups to go right to the top. If you're upset about the destruction of the Amazon, now you can write directly to the leader of Brazil for under a half dollar. If you desire to express support for recent changes in eastern Europe, you can now do so directly to the leaders of those respective nations.

The fact that *How to Write to World Leaders* is, in effect, a targeted reference book, it excludes information you may not need (but nevertheless pay for in other books), and yet directs you to more in-depth sources of information at your local library.

In closing, may I encourage you to express yourself? Take the first step, add your opinion to that of tens of thousands of others, and deliver that opinion directly to the doorstep, *wherever* in the world that doorstep may be.

Mark West
WestMark Associates, March 1991

Introduction

A long time ago, Earth's peoples decided to cooperate and build a tower to heaven. God didn't particularly like this plan, and thwarted it by causing everyone to begin speaking different languages.

With no way to communicate, cooperation was virtually impossible, and the Tower of Babel was abandoned.

Today, the situation has not improved measurably. We are still a world of differing languages, customs, religions, and goals.

Today, however—well, today the world is shrinking. The internal affairs of one nation are no longer a singular concern of that nation; those actions affect the people of many nations.

The destruction of tropical rain forests and the resultant extinction of species concern everyone on earth.

The use of chlorofluorocarbons by one nation may deplete the ozone layer and cause death and destruction the world over.

Recent changes in eastern Europe have affected almost the entire planet. A short time ago, it would have been unthinkable to imagine a united Germany, a disbanding Soviet Union, many nations at war with Iraq. But these things have happened.

Along with millions of others around the world, I watched with dismay the violence in The People's Republic of China during the Spring of 1989. I felt the anger and a desire to *do* something— and then it occurred to me: why not write China's leaders a letter expressing my personal outrage? It was my search for a suitable address that led to this book.

Libraries had reference materials that listed world leaders, and some of them even had addresses. But there was no concise, consistent source of information about world leaders that included mailing addresses.

And because of their size and expense, most of those reference guides are only available at libraries. I wanted a small, targeted reference guide that listed world leaders, their mailing addresses, and, where possible, their phone numbers.

You hold the result of my efforts. Searching the pages that follow can open the entire world to *your* ideas, *your* opinions, *your* concerns.

The world is shrinking. The planet is girdled with computer networks, electronic mail, and FAX machines. Communication is instantaneous via satellite.

Engineers are developing suborbital, supersonic passenger aircraft capable of making transoceanic flights in just a few hours.

Yet communication is still a problem. We have too little tolerance for the customs, religions, and ideas of others.

Communicating is one way to increase understanding.

As a citizen of the world, you are no doubt becoming more and more aware of this "shrinkage." *Your* situation (and responsibility) as a citizen of a particular nation is becoming balanced by your situation (and responsibility) as a citizen of the world.

You're accustomed to communicating your opinions, ideas, feelings and protests to the leaders of your nation. Some peoples of the world have few privileges in such discourse with their nation's leaders.

Between nations, communication is largely restricted to heads of government. The average citizen seldom has ready access to the leaders of other nations.

Until now, there has been no reference that put the names *and* mailing addresses of planet Earth's leaders into the hands of its people.

If you don't like what's going on somewhere in the world, fire off a letter to that nation's leader.

If you have an idea for world peace, *your* opinion can drift across the desks of the appropriate kings, queens, sultans, presidents or prime ministers.

Perhaps the most effective pressure that can be applied to a recalcitrant government is that of public opinion. And what better way to influence public opinion than in a deluge of outraged letters from people all over the world?

A simple book of names and addresses, a compilation of information from many sources—can it be a key to better relations? Improved human rights?

Only time—and perhaps the hand of God—will tell.

How to Use This Book

How to Write to World Leaders has been designed for quick reference, and allows you to easily locate the leader of a particular nation, along with his or her address.

The first part of the book consists of an alphabetical listing of all nations of the world, along with each nation's leader(s), title(s) and mailing address(es). In many cases, a phone number is also provided, and even a few FAX numbers.

Following the alphabetical listing of nations is an alphabetical listing of the leaders, cross-referenced with their respective nations. You will note that in the nation's listing, the leader's last name is in **bold type**. Not all cultures have the same surname custom as your nation. Many Asian countries, for instance, reverse the order as compared to Western custom. Thus, for the sake of clarity, we've indicated with bold type the leader's last name.

In instances where two nations have similar names, or different names refer to two nations, this information is noted below.

For instance, China actually refers to two nations: THE PEOPLE'S REPUBLIC OF CHINA and THE REPUBLIC OF CHINA. The listing for CHINA includes both.

Check the following:

For IVORY COAST see: **CÔTE D'IVORIE.**

For TAIWAN see: Republic of **CHINA** ("C").

For GERMANY see: Federal Republic of **GERMANY** ("G").

For NORTH KOREA see: Democratic People's Republic of **KOREA** ("K").

For SOUTH KOREA see: Republic of **KOREA** ("K").

Territories and protectorates are listed with their parent nations.

Also included in the book are a few of the more prominent international organizations, with a contact person and a mailing address, and one or two prominent people who are world leaders but not necessarily leaders of particular nations.

Listed at the end of this book are some of the reference titles we used in compiling the information. In most cases, we used information verified directly by the nations themselves (or via their embassies in Washington, D.C., or New York City).

A word about name spelling: The recent interest in Iraq has caused several people to question the spelling of the names of certain leaders (including Iraq's President, Saddam Husayn). For the most part, our source for spelling is the Central Intelligence Agency publication, *Chiefs of State and Cabinet Members of Foreign Governments*. That publication contains the following statement:

"The spelling of personal names in this directory follow transliteration systems generally agreed upon by government agencies, except when officials use or have stated a preference for alternate spellings of their names, or when the news media or official documents issued by an individual's country use an alternative spelling."

Letter Writing Tips

People write letters for different reasons. One is probably motivated to write a world leader by anger, a perceived injustice, a perceived brilliant idea, or some other agreement or disagreement with an action by a particular head of government.

Others prefer going "right to the top" seeking information. Some enjoy collecting autographs. Students may choose to write a world leader as a class project. Groups and organizations may wish to forward petitions or other information.

Your motivation and subject matter determine how you might approach writing a letter to a world leader. Below are some tips to help you get your point across.

Remember, in many cases, you will be corresponding with a person who does not write or speak the same language that you do, who grew up and lives in a culture different from your own, and who rules a country with laws, a political philosophy, and problems that may differ tremendously from yours. You must take all these things into consideration when you compose your letter.

1. Make sure the address is copied from this book correctly. In many cases, the postal worker in the destination country does not read your language. Therefore, it's best to type the address, if at all possible.

2. Current U.S. postage rates are as follows (Check your post office for changes):

- Letters to Canada are 40¢ per ounce.

- Mail to Mexico costs 35¢ for up to a half-ounce and 45¢ up to one ounce.

- For other foreign countries, the rate is 50¢ per *half-ounce*. In most cases, two sheets of paper and a business size envelope will weigh in under a half-ounce.

- Aerogrammes cost 45¢ each. You cannot enclose anything inside an aerogramme.

3. When writing your letter, take some time to present your thoughts politely, logically, and in simple, direct and clear language.

4. If at all possible, type your letter and make sure your spelling and punctuation are correct. Often, if your letter reaches the desk of the world leader, it will have been translated into his or her language by a staff member. A typewritten missive makes this translation much easier. For the same reasons, avoid the use of slang and expletives, they may not be known to the translator. If you can't type the letter, print neatly. Handwriting is difficult to read, no matter how excellent your penmanship, and should be avoided.

5. Keep your sentences short and to the point. A short letter with a few main points is much more likely to reach its intended party than a long, rambling letter with many thoughts and points.

6. Restrain your anger, no matter how well-deserved, if that is the purpose of your communication. A polite, logical presentation will have more of an impact than a hysterical blast of hate. But don't hesitate to firmly state your case, express your outrage, or even demand an explanation if you feel such is warranted.

7. Be aware that responses will vary. You may not receive a reply at all. Often, a reply will come from a staff member. Rarely will you receive a personal reply from the leader directly. Don't be discouraged by this—your opinions *will* most likely reach the leader regardless.

9

8. It's also possible that your letter may get lost in transit. The efficiency of postal workers varies tremendously from country to country. Labor actions may delay your letter, political upheavals may intercept it, as may an unscrupulous postal worker who collects foreign stamps (to him or her, *your* stamps are foreign.) For this reason, you may wish to use standard nondescript stamps rather than commemoratives.

9. For best results, use the following format for typing or printing addresses on your envelopes:

   Name and title of the leader

   Office of the leader

   Street address or box number

   City and code (if any)

   COUNTRY

   For clarity's sake, the name of the country should be capitalized. If you're mailing from the United States, postal regulations require that the country be in English. Don't forget your return address, both on the envelope and somewhere on the letter. If you wish to send your letter via registered mail, contact your local post office for details and costs.

10. Avoid the use of form letters and those fill-in-the-blank letters and cards used by many organizations. These efforts have very little impact. An individual, personalized letter in your own words is a much better way to present your opinions. A form letter may sound polished and powerful—but it's really an indication that you don't have the determination to do your own thinking.

11. Be prepared to wait. Not only is your letter subject to the whims of fate and postal clerks, but delivery is often excruciatingly slow. Add more time if your letter needs to be translated. A response within two months is an indication that everything went smoothly.

12. Autograph collectors should avoid writing a letter that merely requests the leader's autograph. This wastes the leader's time and the time of his or her staff. Wait until you have something substantive to share. That way, if you receive a reply, the contents and the signature will be of equal interest.

13. If you're writing about something of deep concern to you, don't write blind. Do some research beforehand. Reference librarians can help you to unearth information about the world leader you're intending to write. Libraries often carry foreign newspapers, which will allow you to gauge the political and social climate of the nation that interests you. The same reference materials can fill you in on the nation's economic and environmental status, its industrial, tourist, and religious perspectives. See the reference listing at the end of this book for examples of where to look.

14. Perhaps most important of all—be persistent. If you're fighting for human rights, or environmental reasons, enlist your friends in writing letters; contact organizations with similar interests and encourage them to begin writing (not form letters, please!).

Make no mistake about it—public opinion has a significant impact. But it's not effective if it lies dormant and unspoken, if it never reaches the decision-makers. With *How to Write to World Leaders* in hand, get your opinions in the mail.

I often wonder if it would have made a difference in China if, shortly after the massacre in 1989, the leaders of that nation had begun receiving tens of thousands of letters every day, day in and day out, expressing anger and outrage for their actions. There's no way to tell, of course, but I wonder . . .

Keeping Your Book Current

How to Write to World Leaders is a reference book. Like virtually all such books, it will, at least in some respects, be outdated before it leaves the printing press.

Change is inevitable. Change among government leaders is constant. There is nothing that can be done about this situation. There are several things that can be done, however, that will increase the useful life of this particular volume.

While we have made every effort to confirm the accuracy of the information in this book, mistakes do occur.

Moreover, world leaders are human beings and not institutions. Leaders are voted out of office, they resign, they are assassinated, they're deposed, overthrown—and sometimes they die.

Fortunately, while leaders do change, addresses usually remain the same (unless, of course, someone opposed to that particular leader blows up the presidential palace).

It doesn't matter who is president of the United States, for instance; he or she will occupy the White House.

By keeping aware of current affairs, you can greatly and easily extend the useful life of this book. You can also utilize the same sources of information we do: news reports, public (or university) libraries, embassies, and the addresses in this book.

With these measures, your copy of *How to Write to World Leaders* will maintain its usefulness much longer than the average reference book.

If a letter you write to a world leader is ever returned as undeliverable, we would like to know. With your help, we can keep our information current.

Also, we'd like to hear about any successes you've had in communicating with world leaders (perhaps you might even send us photocopies of the letter you sent and the response, providing the content is not of an extremely personal nature).

We want *How to Write to World Leaders* to be a useful book over a long period of time. We welcome your suggestions for improving subsequent editions.

What to Do
if It Doesn't Work

Let's say you dutifully send off a letter to a world leader, using the address supplied in this book,—and, months later, you get it back with that familiar finger pointing at your return address.

Your letter is undeliverable as addressed.

What happened?

There are several possibilities. The most obvious is that the wrong address was listed in this book (surprising as it may sound, we *do* make mistakes). In order to determine exactly what went wrong:

- Check to make sure you copied it from the book correctly.
- Check to make sure you affixed sufficient postage.
- Check your local library to make sure that particular nation is not embroiled in a revolution, coup, or some other upheaval that might suspend mail service.
- Check with your local post office to see if the country you're writing to is having labor problems regarding its postal delivery system.

If everything checks out, you'll have to come up with an alternative address. This involves a bit of research, and your local

14

reference librarian can help. Some of the books you might use are listed at the end of this book.

One of those is *The Europa Yearbook*, a large, two-volume reference on every nation on earth, published by Europa Publications Limited, England. Many libraries have it in their reference collections, and it contains a wealth of information and address possibilities. Try writing in care of the nation's embassy.

Several reference books list addresses of local embassies. Most countries have United Nations addresses (even nations that have no formal diplomatic ties with the United States). You'll also find listings for other governmental offices within the country you're writing. You may wish to send your letter in care of a minister of foreign affairs, perhaps, or the minister of information (and/or communication).

Countries normally have embassies in many nations. If your country does not have an embassy for the country you're writing, try writing an embassy in a third nation.

Also, while you're at it, let us know that your letter failed to get through. We'll attempt to ascertain what went wrong, and correct the situation.

Suggested Projects

Classes, organizations, groups, and individuals can make use of *How to Write to World Leaders* in a variety of ways. Below are some suggested projects. If our projects seem to you to be somewhat grandiose in concept, you can scale them down, depending upon your resources, motivation, and time.

The important aspect is doing something, not how much is done.

Filling a Need Project

Utilizing various methods and skills, participants investigate, research, and select a country, and a need within that country, then work to begin filling that need.

1. Assign a group to maintain the current status of this book. This group would be charged with checking daily newspapers, reports, and other sources to make corrections when changes in leadership occur.

2. Assign a group to choose a geographic area of the planet to focus on. This group would then make specific recommendations regarding the country to be contacted, with the final choice to be made by the entire group.

3. Assign a group to conduct research on the selected nation in order to determine a particular need of the citizens of that country (e.g., textbooks, farm implements, clothing, medical supplies, etc.). For this example, we'll propose sending textbooks to an elementary school. This group would also locate additional addresses appropriate to the project, including the country's embassy in the United States.

4. Assign a group to set and outline steps that must be met to accomplish the goal. If the project requires funds, fund-raising must be considered. If, for instance, the project consists of sending textbooks to a school in the selected nation, you'll have to be concerned with several questions: Where do the books come from, what are the postal regulations and mailing requirements, what is the address of the target school, and what is the cost?

5. Write to the leader of the selected nation, suggesting one or more of the projects your group wishes to accomplish during the time available. At the same time, send letters to the other addresses secured by the research group. Move ahead without waiting for an answer. Initiate contact with the school in order to determine what textbooks are needed. If no answer is received from the school or the nation's leader within a reasonable time (say, three months), assign a group to call the embassy, or contact the U.S. Department of State for assistance.

6. Assign a group to publicize the project to the media, including local papers and broadcast media as well as networks and wire services. This should help with fund-raising activities.

7. Once the nation's leader or representative has responded, or you have secured sufficient information to accomplish the goal, proceed with the project to its completion.

8. Make sure to report your success to the media. Members of individual groups should meet to assess the overall project and prepare a report for the participants in whole. Consider making a successful project an ongoing one.

Righting a Wrong Project

Participants determine a global problem and work to lend their weight in resolving that problem.

1. Assign a group to determine the goal of the project, some wrong that urgently needs to be addressed. For example, countries that still allow whaling, or those that promote destruction of rain forests, might be encouraged to change their practices. We'll use whaling for this example.

2. Assign a group to secure information about the project, and why it is wrong. For instance, members can contact organizations and groups opposed to whaling for information. Query the U.S. government on its policies; the Department of the Interior and the Department of State will probably be the most helpful.

3. Assign a group to identify nations that still allow whaling, and determine the target nation. Research that nation's rationalization for whaling so that counterarguments may be devised.

4. Assign a group to do publicity. You can approach this problem by limiting letter writing to the group, or by starting a letter writing campaign among the general public in your town or school district. If you choose the former, you want publicity for the group. Write-ups in the local press and interviews on local television or radio stations provide excellent motivation.

5. If you choose a general letter writing campaign, you need to address several areas of publicity. Try to get permission for students to distribute flyers at local shopping malls. Contact local media for their help in encouraging the public to write.

6. Using the names and addresses in this book, have the group prepare individual letters to mail, and provide these addresses to members of the public who choose to write.

7. As an added impetus, assign a group to secure the names and addresses of newspapers and television stations in the selected nation, and contact them also. If you get publicity in the target country, your campaign will be much more effective—and may receive international publicity.

8. Assign a group to prepare a report on the effectiveness of public opinion, and on some recent effective letter writing campaigns. Use this as a kickoff point to assess the group's effectiveness in accomplishing the goals of the project.

9. Share any responses from the nation's leader with local media.

Eastern Europe—
Compare and Contrast

Participants conduct research on recent changes in eastern Europe, and gather current information in order to compare and contrast current government practices with former ones.

1. Assign a group to research and study recent changes in eastern European nations. Have them recommend three or four nations for closer study and contact.

2. Assign a group to compare and contrast the forms of government these nations have had since the turn of the century with governmental philosophy that is current or in formation today. What kinds of political and economic problems do the citizens of these nations face?

3. Write to the leaders of these nations to discuss the differing forms of government, and to inquire about future plans, problems, and possible solutions. It may be necessary to write not only to the leaders of these nations, but also their embassies in the United States.

4. Have a group contact a university or media expert on eastern Europe and ask for authoratative comment on the information derived by the group from the nations queried.

5. Collect all information gathered, including responses from the nations themselves, the experts, and the research, and produce a "white paper" report on the recent changes in eastern Europe, and hopes for the future.

6. Hold a press conference to release the "white paper" report. Be sure to send the leaders of the nations involved a copy of the report. Copies should also go to appropriate local, state, and federal officials.

Adopt a Leader Project

This one will probably work best with one of the smaller nations. Participants select and "adopt" a world leader for the duration of the available time period (school year, semester, etc.), sharing with him or her information and accomplishments and requesting information in return.

1. Assign a group to research and prepare recommendations on several nations, profiling their leaders and suggesting one for "adoption" by the group.

2. Have the group vote on the nation and the leader to be "adopted", and the goals to be accomplished.

3. Write a class letter to the leader, informing him or her of your plans and exactly what being adopted means (as determined by the group).

4. Assign groups to chronicle the class, interview classmates, research the roots of local traditions and culture in order to prepare a series of reports, letters, and news accounts about the group and the environment in which it exists.

5. Assign a group to do in-depth research on the selected nation, so that comparisons and contrasts may be made in correspondence with the "adopted" leader. Select a special project that will be presented as a gift to the leader (perhaps a mural of the group's home town or its perceptions of the leader's nation).

6. Encourage individual group members to write weekly or monthly letters to the leader, sharing whatever ideas they wish. Someone should take photos to send.

7. Plan a cultural day in which group members adopt the dress and food and culture of the leader's nation. Make sure to send him or her pictures of the event.

The above examples are merely suggestions. There are many more possibilities—some simple, others more complex—for the accomplishment of large groups or individuals. Imagination is the only limiting factor.

Key to Abbreviations

Adm.—Admiral
Brig.-Gen.—Brigadier General
Capt.—Captain
Col.—Colonel
Dr.—Doctor
Flight-Lt.—Flight Lieutenant
Gen.—General
HE—His/Her Excellency
HH—His/Her Highness
HM—His/Her Majesty
HRH—His/Her Royal Highness
HSH—His/Her Serene Highness
Lt.-Col.—Lieutenant Colonel
Lt.-Gen.—Lieutenant General
Maj.—Major
Maj.-Gen.—Major General
Ret.—Retired

Leaders of the Earth's Nations

Republic of
AFGHANISTAN
(southwestern Asia)

Dr. **Najibullah**, President
Office of the President
Kabul
AFGHANISTAN
Telephone: 25889
FAX:26340

Fazil Haq **Khaliqyar**, Prime Minister
Char Rahi Sedarat
Kabul
AFGHANISTAN
Telephone: (93) 24355

People's Socialist Republic of
ALBANIA
(southeastern Europe)

Ylli Sokrat **Bufi**, Premier
Office of the Premier
Tirana
ALBANIA

Ramiz **Alia**, President
Office of the President
Tirana
ALBANIA

Democratic and Popular Republic
of
ALGERIA
(northern Africa)

Col. **Bendjedid** Chadli, President
Présidence de la République
El-Mouradia
Algiers
ALGERIA
Telephone: 60-03-60

Sid Ahmed **Ghozal**, Prime Minister
Office of the Prime Minister
Palais du Gouvernement
Algiers
ALGERIA
Telephone: 60-23-40

ANDORRA
(western Europe)

Josef Pintat **Solans**, President of Government
Office of the President
Andorra la Vella
ANDORRA

People's Republic of
ANGOLA
(western coast of Africa)

José Eduardo dos **Santos**, President
Office of the President
Luanda
ANGOLA

ANTIGUA and BARBUDA
(West Indies)

Vere C. **Bird**, Sr., Prime Minister
Office of the Prime Minister
Factory Road
St. John's
ANTIGUA
Telephone: (809) 462-0773/0779

ARGENTINA

(South America)

Carlos Saul **Menem**, President
Office of the President
Balcarce 50
1064 Buenos Aires
ARGENTINA
Telephone: (1) 46-9841

Commonwealth of
AUSTRALIA

(Indian and Pacific Oceans)

Robert J.L. **Hawke**, Prime Minister
Office of the Prime Minister
Edmund Barton Building
Macquarie Street
Barton ACT 2600
Canberra
AUSTRALIA
Telephone: (062) 723955

Republic of
AUSTRIA
(central Europe)

Dr. Kurt **Waldheim**, Federal President
Office of the President
A-1010 Wien
Ballhausplatz 1
Hofburg
AUSTRIA
FAX: 5356512

Franz **Vranitzky**, Federal Chancellor
Office of the Federal Chancellor
Bundeshanzleramt
A-1014 Wien
Ballhausplatz 2
AUSTRIA
FAX: 5350-338

The Commonwealth of the
THE BAHAMAS
(West Indies)

Sir Lynden Oscar **Pindling**, Prime Minister
Office of the Prime Minister
P.O. Box N-3733
Rawson Sq.
Nassau
THE BAHAMAS
Telephone: 322-2805

State of
BAHRAIN
(Persian Gulf)

Sheikh Isa bin Sulman al-**Khalifa**, Amir
Amiri Court
P.O. Box 555
Riffa Palace
Manama
BAHRAIN
Telephone: 661-252

Sheikh Khalifa bin Salman al-**Khalifa**, Prime Minister
Office of the Prime Minister
P.O. Box 1000
Government House
Government Road
Manama
BAHRAIN
Telephone: 262-266

People's Republic of
BANGLADESH
(southern Asia)

Shahabuddin **Ahmed**, President
President's Secretariat
Old Sangsad Bhaban
Dhaka
BANGLADESH
Telephone: 310111-5

Khaleda **ZIAur** Rahman, Prime Minister
Prime Minister's Secretariat
Sher-e-Bangla Nagar
Dhaka
BANGLADESH
Telephone: 328292

BARBADOS
(West Indies)

Rt. Hon. Lloyd Erskine **Sandiford**, Prime Minister
Office of the Prime Minister
Government Headquarters
Bay Street
St. Michael
BARBADOS
Telephone: 436-6435

Kingdom of
BELGIUM
(northwestern Europe)

HM King **Baudouin** I, King of the Belgians
Palais Royal
B-1000 Bruxelles
BELGIUM

Dr. Wilfried **Martens**, Prime Minister
Office of the Prime Minister
16 rue de la Loi
1000 Brussels
BELGIUM
Telephone: (02) 513-80-20

BELIZE
(Caribbean coast of Central America)

George **Price**, Prime Minister
Office of the Prime Minister
Belmopan
BELIZE
Telephone: 08-2346

Republic of
BENIN
(western Africa)

Nicephore **Soglo**, President
Office of the President
BP 2028
Cotonou
BENIN
Telephone: 30-00-90

Kingdom of
BHUTAN
(south central Asia)

HM Jigme Singye **Wangchuck**, King of Bhutan
Office of the King
The Royal Secretariat
Tashichhodzong
Thimphu
BHUTAN
Telephone: 22521
FAX: 975 22079

Republic of
BOLIVIA
(South America)

Jaime **Paz Zamora**, President
Office of the President
Palacio de Gobierno
Plaza Murillo
La Paz
BOLIVIA
Telephone: (2) 371317

Republic of
BOTSWANA
(southern Africa)

Dr. Quett Ketumile Joni **Masire**, President
State House
Private Bag 001
Gaborone
BOTSWANA
Telephone: 355444

Federative Republic of
BRAZIL
(central South America)

Fernando **Collor** de Mello, President
Office of the President
Palácio do Planalto
Praca dos Trés Poderes
70.150 Brasília, DF
BRAZIL
Telephone: (061)-211-1221
FAX: (61)-226-7566

BRUNEI
(southeastern Asia)

HM Sir Muda Haji **Hassanal** Bolkiah Mu'izzaddin Waddaulah, Sultan and Yang Di-Pertuan and Prime Minister
Office of the Sultan and Prime Minister
Istana Nurul Iman
Bandar Seri Begawan 1100
BRUNEI
Telephone: (02) 229988

Republic of
BULGARIA
(southeastern Europe)

Zhelyu **Zhelev**, President
Office of the President
Blvd. Dondukov 1
1000 Sofia
BULGARIA
Telephone: 887-2241
FAX: 803418

Dimiter **Popov**, Chairman, Council of Ministers
(Premier)
Office of the Premier
Blvd. Dondukov 2
1000 Sofia
BULGARIA

BURKINA FASO
(western Africa)

Capt. Blaise **Campaoré**, Chairman of the Popular Front
Office of the Chairman
Ouagadougou
BURKINA FASO

Union of
BURMA
(southeastern Asia)

Gen. **Saw Maung**, Chairman, State Law & Order
Restoration Council
Office of the Chairman
Ady Road
Rangoon
BURMA
Telephone: (01) 60776

Republic of
BURUNDI
(central Africa)

Maj. Pierre **Buyoya**, President
Office of the President
Bujumbura
BURUNDI
Telephone: 6063

Adrien **Sibomana**, Prime Minister
Office of the Prime Minister
Bujumbura
BURUNDI

CAMBODIA
(southeastern Asia)

Norodom Sihanouk, President
Office of the President
Phnom-Penh
CAMBODIA

Hun Sen, Prime Minister
Office of the Prime Minister
Phnom-Penh
CAMBODIA

Republic of
CAMEROON
(western coast of Africa)

P.M. Sadou **Hayatou**, President
Office of the President
Central Post Office
Yaoundé
CAMEROON
Telephone: 23-40-25

CANADA
(northern North America)

(Martin) Brian **Mulroney**, Prime Minister
Office of the Prime Minister
Langevin Blk.
Ottawa, Ontario K1A 0A2
CANADA
Telephone: (613) 992-4211

Republic of
CAPE VERDE
(central Atlantic Ocean)

Antonio Montiero **Mascarenhas**, President
Office of the President
Presidência da República
Praia
São Tiago
CAPE VERDE
Telephone: 260

Carlos Alberto Wahnon de Carvalho **Veiga**,
Prime Minister
Office of the Prime Minister
Praca 12 de Setembro
CP 16
Praia
São Tiago
CAPE VERDE
Telephone: 248

CENTRAL AFRICAN REPUBLIC
(central Africa)

Gen. André-Dieudonne **Kolingba**, President
Office of the President
Palais de la Renaissance
Bangui
CENTRAL AFRICAN REPUBLIC
Telephone: 61-03-23

Edouard **Franck**, Prime Minister
Office of the Prime Minister
Bangui
CENTRAL AFRICAN REPUBLIC

Republic of CHAD
(northcentral Africa)

Idriss **Deby**, President
Office of the President
N'Djamena
CHAD
Telephone: 514437

Jean Bawoyeu **Alingue**, Prime Minister
Office of the Prime Minister
N'Djamena
CHAD

Republic of
CHILE
(Pacific coast of South America)

Patricio **Aylwin** Azocar, President
Office of the President
Palacio de la Moneda
Santiago
CHILE
Telephone: (562) 714103/717054

The People's Republic of
CHINA
(eastern Asia)

Yang Shangkun, President
Office of the President
Zhonganahai
Beijing
PEOPLE'S REPUBLIC OF CHINA

Li Peng, Premier, State Council
Office of the Premier
Zhonganahai
Beijing
PEOPLE'S REPUBLIC OF CHINA

Jiang Zemin, Chairman, Central Military Command
Office of the Chairman
Zhonganahai
Beijing
PEOPLE'S REPUBLIC OF CHINA

Republic of
CHINA (TAIWAN)
(southeastern coast of Mainland China)

Lee Teng-Hui, President
Office of the President
Chieh-Shou Hall
Chung-King South Road
Taipei
Taiwan
REPUBLIC OF CHINA
Telephone: (02) 311-3731

Republic of
COLOMBIA
(northwestern South America)

Cesar **Gaviria** Trujillo, President
Office of the President
Bogotá
COLOMBIA

Federal Islamic Republic of
THE COMOROS
(Mozambique Channel)

Said Mohamed **Djohar**, President
Office of the President
BP 421
Moroni
THE COMOROS
Telephone: 2413

People's Republic of
THE CONGO
(western coast of Africa)

Gen. Denis **Sassou-Nguesso**, President
Office of the President
Palais du Peuple
Brazzaville
THE CONGO

Andre **Milongo**, Prime Minister
Office of the Prime Minister
Brazzaville
THE CONGO

Republic of
COSTA RICA
(Central America)

Rafael Angel **Calderón** Fournier, President
Casa Presidencial
Apdo 520
Zapote
San José
COSTA RICA
Telephone: 244092

Republique de
CÔTE D'IVOIRE (The Ivory Coast)
(western coast of Africa)

Dr. Félix **Houphouët-Boigny**, President
Office of the President
Abidjan
CÔTE D'IVOIRE

Alassane **Ouattara**, Prime Minister
Office of the Prime Minister
Abidjan
CÔTE D'IVOIRE

Republic of
CUBA
(Caribbean Sea)

Dr. Fidel **Castro** Ruz, President
Office of the President
Consejo de Estado
Plaza de la Revolución
Ciudad de la Habana
CUBA

Republic of
CYPRUS
(eastern Mediterranean Sea)

George **Vassiliou**, President
Office of the President
Presidential Palace
Nicosia
CYPRUS

CZECH AND SLOVAK FEDERAL REPUBLIC

(central Europe)

Vaclav **Havel**, President
Office of the President
119 08 Praha 1-Hrad
Prague
CZECHOSLOVAKIA
Telephone: (02) 2101 or 534541
FAX: (02) 535674, 3112281

Marián **Calfa**, Prime Minister
Office of the Prime Minister
Nábr. kpt Jarose 4
125 09 Praha 1
Prague
CZECHOSLOVAKIA
Telephone: (02) 2102 or 539041
FAX: (02) 2365260, 2369473

Kingdom of
DENMARK
(northern Europe)

HM Queen **Margrethe II**, Queen of Denmark
Office of the Queen
Amalienborg Palace
Copenhagen k.
DENMARK

Poul **Schlüter**, Prime Minister
Office of the Prime Minister
Christiansborg Palace
Prins Jørgens Gaard II
1218 Copenhagen k.
DENMARK
Telephone: (01) 4533923300

Republic of
DJIBOUTI
(Horn of Africa)

Hassan Gouled Aptidon, President of the Republic
Office of the President
Djibouti
DJIBOUTI

Barkat Gourad Hamadou, Prime Minister
Office of the Prime Minister
BP 2086
DJIBOUTI
Telephone: 351494

Commonwealth of
DOMINICA
(West Indies)

Sir Clarence Augustus **Seignoret**, President
Office of the President
Victoria Street
Roseau
DOMINICA
Telephone: 82054

Mary Eugenia **Charles**, Prime Minister
Office of the Prime Minister
Government Headquarters
Kennedy Avenue
Roseau
DOMINICA
Telephone: 809-448-2401 to 6

THE DOMINICAN REPUBLIC
(Carribbean Sea)

Dr. Joaquín **Balaguer** Ricardo, President
Office of the President
Santo Domingo
THE DOMINICAN REPUBLIC

Republic of
ECUADOR
(western coast of South America)

Rodrigo **Borja** Cevallos, President
Office of the President
Palacio Nacional
Garciá Moreno 1043
Quito
ECUADOR
Telephone: 216-300

Arab Republic of
EGYPT
(northeastern Africa)

Mohammed Hosni **Mubarak**, President
Office of the President
Cairo
EGYPT

Dr. Atef **Sedky**, Prime Minister
Office of the Prime Minister
Cairo
EGYPT

Republic of
EL SALVADOR
(Central America)

(Felix) Alfredo **Cristiani** Buckard, President
Office of the President
Casa Presidencial
San Salvador
EL SALVADOR

Republic of
EQUATORIAL GUINEA
(western coast of Africa)

Brig.-Gen. Teodoro **Obiang Nquema Mbasogo**,
President
Office of the President
Malabo
EQUATORIAL GUINEA

ESTONIA
(northern Europe)

Arnold F. **Rüütel**, Chairman
Office of the Chairman
Tallinn
ESTONIA

People's Democratic Republic of
ETHIOPIA
(eastern Africa)

Meles Zenawi, Acting President
Office of the President
Addis Ababa
ETHIOPIA

(currently vacant)
Office of the Prime Minister
P.O. Box 1013
Addis Ababa
ETHIOPIA
Telephone: 123400

FAROE ISLANDS
(Danish External Territory)

Faroe Islands Home Government
Atli **Dam**, Prime Minister
Tinganes
P. O. Box 64
FR-100 Torshavn
FAROE ISLANDS
Telephone: 298 110 80

Republic of
FIJI
(Pacific Ocean)

Ratu Sir Penaia **Ganilau**, President
Office of the President
Suva
FIJI

Kamisese **Mara**, Prime Minister
Office of the Prime Minister
Suva
FIJI
Telephone: 211-201

Republic of
FINLAND
(northern Europe)

Dr. Mauno **Koivisto**, President
Office of the President
Mariankatu 2
00170 Helsinki
FINLAND
Telephone: 0 661 133

Esko **Aho**, Prime Minister
Prime Minister's Office
Aleksanterinkatu 30
00170 Helsinki
FINLAND
Telephone: (90) 1601

FRANCE
(western Europe)

François **Mitterrand**, President
Office of the President
Palais de l'Elysée
55-57 rue du Faubourg Saint Honoré
75008 Paris
FRANCE
Telephone: (1) 42-92-81-00

Edith **Cresson**, Prime Minister
Office of the Prime Minister
Hôtel de Matignon
57, rue de Varenne
75700 Paris
FRANCE
Telephone: (1) 42-75-80-00
FAX (1) 45-44-15-72

FRENCH TERRITORIES
(southern Pacific Ocean)

FRENCH POLYNESIA

Jean **Montpezat**, High Commissioner
High Commissioner's Office
Papeete
FRENCH POLYNESIA
Telephone: 568.42.20.00
FAX 689.42.37.18

NEW CALEDONIA

Bernard **Grasset**, High Commissioner
High Commissioner's Office
Nouméa
NEW CALEDONIA
Telephone: 687.27.28.22
FAX: 687.27.28.28

GABON
(western coast of Africa)

El Hadj Omar (Albert-Bernard) **Bongo**, President
Office of the President
Libreville
GABON

Casimir **Oye-Mba**, Prime Minister
Office of the Prime Minister
BP 546
Libreville
GABON

Republic of
THE GAMBIA
(western coast of Africa)

Alhaji Sir Dawda Kairaba **Jawara**, President
Office of the President
State House
Banjul
THE GAMBIA
Telephone: 27208

Federal Republic of
GERMANY (FRG)
(Europe)

Dr. Richard von **Weizsäcker**, Federal President
Office of the Federal President
Bundesprsidialamt
Kaiser-Friedrich str. 16-18
D-5300 Bonn 1
FEDERAL REPUBLIC OF GERMANY
Telephone: 011/49/228/2000
FAX: 011/49/228/200200 or 228/200300

Dr. Helmut **Kohl**, Federal Chancellor
Office of the Federal Chancellor
Bundeskanzleramt
Adenauerallee 139-141
D-5300 Bonn 1
FEDERAL REPUBLIC OF GERMANY
Telephone: 011/49/228/561
FAX: 011/49/228/56-23 57

Republic of
GHANA
(western coast of Africa)

Flight-Lt. (Ret.) Jerry John **Rawlings**, Chairman of the
Provisional National Defense Council
Office of the Chairman
Accra
GHANA

GREECE
(southeastern Europe)

Constantinos **Karamanlis**, President
Presidential Palace
7 Vas. Georgiou B' Street
Athens
GREECE
Telephone: (01) 724 8721

Constantinos **Mitsotakis**, Prime Minister
Office of the Prime Minister
Greek Parliament
Athens
GREECE
Telephone: (01) 323 8434

GREENLAND
(Danish External Territory)

Lars **Emil**, Prime Minister
Greenland Home Rule Government
P. O. Box 1015
3900 Nuuk
GREENLAND
Telephone: (009) 299-230-00

GRENADA
(West Indies)

Nicholas A. **Brathwaite**, Prime Minister
Office of the Prime Minister
St. George's
GRENADA
Telephone: 2255
FAX: (809) 440-4116

Republic of
GUATEMALA
(Central America)

Jorge **Serrano** Elias, President
Office of the President
Palacio Nacional
Guatemala City
GUATEMALA
Telephone: 011-502-2-21-2-12

Republic of
GUINEA
(western coast of Africa)

Gen. Lansana **Conté**, President
Office of the President
Conakry
GUINEA
Telephone: 44-11-47

Republic of
GUINEA-BISSAU
(western coast of Africa)

Brig.-Gen. Joào Bernardo **Vieira**, President
Office of the President
Bissau
GUINEA-BISSAU

Co-operative Republic of
GUYANA
(northern coast of South America)

Hugh Desmond **Hoyte**, President
Office of the President
New Garden Street
Georgetown
GUYANA
Telephone: 51330

Hamilton **Green**, Prime Minister
Office of the Prime Minister
Georgetown
GUYANA

Republic of
HAITI
(Caribbean Sea)

Joseph **Nerette**, President (unrecognized by OAS)
Office of the President
Palais National
Port-au-Prince
HAITI
Telephone: 22-4020

Republic of
HONDURAS
(Central America)

Rafael Leonardo **Callejas**, President
Casa Presidencial
6a Avda
1a Calle
Tegucigalpa
HONDURAS
Telephone: 22-8287

Republic of
HUNGARY
(eastern Europe)

Arpád **Göncz**, President
Office of the President
V. Kossuth L. tér 1/3.
1055 Budapest
HUNGARY
Telephone: 122-0600
FAX: 153-5542

József **Antall**, Prime Minister
Office of the Prime Minister
V. Kossuth L. tér 1/3.
1055 Budapest
HUNGARY
Telephone: 122-0600
FAX: 153-3622

Republic of
ICELAND
(north Atlantic Ocean)

Vigdís **Finnbogadóttir**, President
Office of the President
150 Reykjavík
ICELAND

David **Oddsson**, Prime Minister
Office of the Prime Minister
Stjo'rnarráoshúsio
v/Læjartorg
150 Reykjavík
ICELAND

Republic of
INDIA
(Asia)

Ramaswamy Iyer **Venkataraman**, President
Office of the President
Rashtrapti Bhavan
New Delhi 110004
INDIA
Telephone: (11) 3015321

Chandra **Shezhar**, Prime Minister
Office of the Prime Minister
South Block
New Delhi 110011
INDIA
Telephone: (11) 3012312

Republic of
INDONESIA
(13,700 Pacific Ocean islands)

Gen. (Ret) **Soeharto**, President
Office of the President
Istana Merdeka
Jakarta
INDONESIA
Telephone (021) 331097

Islamic Republic of
IRAN
(Persian Gulf)

Ali Akbar **Hashemi-Rafsanjani**
Office of the President
Teheran
IRAN

Ali Hoseini-**Khamenei**, Ayatollah
Office of the Ayatollah
Teheran
IRAN

Republic of
IRAQ
(Persian Gulf)

Saddam **Husayn**, President
Presidential Palace
Karradat Mariam
Baghdad
IRAQ

Saadoun **Hammadi**, Prime Minister
Office of the Prime Minister
Karradat Miriam
Baghdad
IRAQ

Republic of
IRELAND
(north Atlantic Ocean)

Mary **Robinson**, President
Office of the President
'Aras an Uachtaráin
Phoenix Park
Dublin 8
IRELAND
Telephone: (01) 772815

Charles J. **Haughey**, Taoiseach (Prime Minister)
Office of An Taoiseach
Government Buildings
Upper Merrion Street
Dublin 2
IRELAND
Telephone: (01) 689333

State of
ISRAEL
(Middle East)

Gen. Chaim **Herzog**, President
Office of the President
Jerusalem
ISRAEL

Yitzhak **Shamir**, Prime Minister
Office of the Prime Minister
Hakirya
Ruppin Street
Jerusalem
ISRAEL

ITALY
(southern Europe)

Francesco **Cossiga**, President of the Republic
Office of the President
Palazzo del Quirinale
00187 Rome
ITALY
Telephone: (06) 4699

Giulio **Andreotti**, Prime Minister
Office of the Prime Minister
Palazzo Chigi
Piazza Colonna 370
00100 Rome
ITALY
Telephone: (06) 6779

JAMAICA
(Caribbean Sea)

Michael **Manley**, Prime Minister
Office of the Prime Minister
1 Devon Road
Kingston 10
JAMAICA
Telephone: 927-9941

JAPAN
(eastern Asia)

HM Emperor **Akihito**
Imperial Household Agency
1-1, Chiyoda
Chiyoda-ku
Tokyo 100
JAPAN
Telephone: (03) 213-1111

Kiichi **Miyazawa**, Prime Minister
Office of the Prime Minister
1-6, Nagata-cho
Chiyoda-ku
Tokyo
JAPAN
Telephone: (3) 581-2361

Hashemite Kingdom of
JORDAN
(Middle East)

HM King **Hussein** Ibn Talal
Royal Palace
Amman
JORDAN

Tahir al-**Masri**, Prime Minister
Office of the Prime Minister
P.O. Box 80
35216 Amman
JORDAN
Telephone: 641211

Republic of
KENYA
(eastern coast of Africa)

Daniel arap **Moi**, President
Office of the President
Harambee House
Harambee Avenue
P.O. Box 30510
Nairobi
KENYA
Telephone: 27411

Republic of
KIRIBATI
(mid-Pacific Ocean)

Teatao **Teannaki**, President
Office of the President
P.O. Box 61
Bairiki
Tarawa
KIRIBATI
Telephone: 21342

Democratic People's Republic of
KOREA
(Asia)

Marshal **Kim** Il-song, President
Office of the President
Pyongyang
NORTH KOREA

Yon Hyong-muk, Premier
Office of the Premier
Pyongyang
NORTH KOREA

Republic of
KOREA
(Asia)

Roh Tae-Woo, President
Office of the President
Chong Wa Dae
1 Sejong-no
Chongno-ku
Seoul
SOUTH KOREA

Chung Won-shik, Prime Minister
Office of the Prime Minister
77 Sejong-no
Chongno-ku
Seoul
SOUTH KOREA
Telephone: 720-2001

State of
KUWAIT
(Persian Gulf)

HH Sheikh Jabir al-Ahmad al-Jabir Al-**Sabah**, Amir of
Kuwait
Office of the Amir
Bayan Palace
KUWAIT

Sheikh Sa`d al-`Abdallah as-Salim Al-**Sabah**, Crown
Prince and Prime Minister
Office of the Prime Minister
Bayan Palace
KUWAIT

LAOS
(southeastern Asia)

Souphanouvong, President
Office of the President
Vientiane
LAOS

Kaysone Phomvihan, Chairman, Council of Ministers
Office of the Chairman
Vientiane
LAOS

LATVIA
(northern Europe)

Anatolijs V. **Gorbunous**, President
Office of the President
Riga
LATVIA

Republic of
LEBANON
(Middle East)

Ilyas **Harawi**, President
Office of the President
Beruit
LEBANON

Omar **Karami**, Prime Minister
Office of the Prime Minister
Beruit
LEBANON

Kingdom of
LESOTHO
(southern Africa)

HM **Letsie** III, King
The Royal Palace
P.O. Box 524
Maseru
LESOTHO
Telephone: 322170

Col. Elias Phisoana **Ramapma**, Head of Government
Office of the Head of Government
Maseru
LESOTHO

Republic of
LIBERIA
(western coast of Africa)

Charles **Taylor**, (self-proclaimed) President*
Office of the President
Monrovia
LIBERIA
*Amos **Sawyer** is President-in-Exile

LIBYA
(northern Africa)

Col. Mu`ammar Abu Minyar al-**Qadhafi**, Revolutionary
Leader
Office of the Revolutionary Leader
Tripoli
LIBYA

Abuzeid Omar **Dorda**, Prime Minister
Office of the Prime Minister
Tripoli
LIBYA

Principality of
LIECHTENSTEIN
(central Europe)

HSH **Hans** Adam II
Schloss
FL-9490 Vaduz
LIECHTENSTEIN

Hans **Brunhart**, Head of Government
Regierungsgebäude
FL-9490 Vaduz
LIECHTENSTEIN

LITHUANIA
(northern Europe)

Vtyautas Z. **Landsbergis**, President
Office of the President
Vilnius
LITHUANIA

Grand Duchy of
LUXEMBOURG
(western Europe)

HRH Grand Duke **Jean** Benoît Guillaume Marie Robert
Louis Antoine
Adolphe Marc d'Aviano, Head of State
Palais Grand-Ducal
1728 Luxembourg
LUXEMBOURG

Jacques **Santer**, Prime Minister
Office of the Prime Minister
Hôtel de Bourgogne
4 rue de la Congrégation
1352 Luxembourg-Ville
LUXEMBOURG
Telephone: 47-81

Democratic Republic of
MADAGASCAR
(western Indian Ocean)

Adm. Didier **Ratsiraka**, President
Office of the President
Antananarivo
MADAGASCAR

Col. Victor **Ramahatra**, Prime Minister
Office of the Prime Minister
Mahazoarivo
Antananarivo
MADAGASCAR
Telephone: 25258

Republic of
MALAWI
(south central Africa)

Dr. Hastings Kamuzu **Banda**, President
Office of the President
Private Bag 388
Capital City
Lilongwe 3
MALAWI

MALAYSIA
(southeastern Asia)

Azlan Muhibbuddin Shah ibni Sultan Yusof Izzudin,
Supreme Head of State
Office of the Supreme Head of State
Kuala Lampur
MALAYSIA

Dr. Mahathir bin **Mohamad**, Prime Minister
Office of the Prime Minister
Jalan Dato Onn
50502 Kuala Lampur
MALAYSIA
Telephone: (03) 2301957

Republic of
MALDIVES
(southern Asia)

Maumoon Abdul **Gayoom**, President and Head of State
The President's Office
Male' 20-05
MALDIVES
Telephone: 323701
FAX: 325500 RIYAASATH

Republic of
MALI
(western Africa)

Amadou Toumani **Toure**, President
Office of the President
BP 1463
Bamako
MALI
Telephone: 22-24-61

Soumana **Sako**, Prime Minister
Office of the Prime Minister
Bamako
MALI

Republic of
MALTA
(southern Europe)

Vincent (Censu) **Tabone**, President of the Republic
Office of the President
The Palace
Valletta
MALTA
Telephone: 231945

Dr. Edward **Fenech-Adami**, Prime Minister
Office of the Prime Minister
Auberge de Castille
Valletta
MALTA
Telephone: 242560
FAX: 234494

Republic of the
MARSHALL ISLANDS
(Pacific Ocean)

Amata **Kabua**, President
Office of the President
Majuro
MARSHALL ISLANDS, MH 96960

Islamic Republic of
MAURITANIA
(northwestern Africa)

Col. Maaouiya Ould Sid'Ahmed **Taya**, President of the
Republic, Chairman of the Military Committee for Na-
tional Salvation and Prime Minister
Office of the President
Présidence de la République
BP 184
Nouakchott
MAURITANIA
Telephone: 523-17

MAURITIUS
(Indian Ocean)

Anerood **Jugnauth**, Prime Minister
Office of the Prime Minister
Government House
Port Louis
MAURITIUS
Telephone: 201-1001

MEXICO
(North and Central America)

Carlos **Salinas** de Gortari, President
Office of the President
El Palacio Nacional
México, DF 06066
MEXICO
Telephone: (905) 515.98.36

Federated States of
MICRONESIA
(Pacific Ocean)

James **Olter**, President
Office of the President
Kolonia, Pohnpei
Eastern Caroline Islands
MICRONESIA, FM 96943

Principality of
MONACO
(western Europe)

HRH Prince **Rainier** III
Office of the Prince
MC 98000
MONACO

Jean **Ausseil**, Minister of State
Office of the Minister of State
MC 98000
MONACO

MONGOLIA
(central Asia)

Punsalmaagiyn **Ochirbat**, President
Office of the Chairman
Ulan Bator
MONGOLIA

Dashiyn **Byambasuren**, Prime Minister
Office of the Prime Minister
Ulan Bator
MONGOLIA

Kingdom of
MOROCCO
(northwestern Africa)

HM King **Hassan** II
Office of the King
Rabat
MOROCCO

Dr. Azzedine **Laraki**, Prime Minister
Office of the Prime Minister
Rabat
MOROCCO

People's Republic of
MOZAMBIQUE
(eastern Coast of Africa)

Joaquím Alberto **Chissano**, President of the Republic and
Commander-in-Chief of the Armed Forces
Office of the President
Auda Julius Nyerere
Maputo
MOZAMBIQUE
Telephone: 741121

Mário da Graça **Machungo**, Prime Minister
Office of the Prime Minister
Maputo
MOZAMBIQUE

Republic of
NAMIBIA
(southwestern Africa)

Sam **Nujoma**, President
Windhoek
Namibia

Hage **Geingob**, Prime Minister
Windhoek
Namibia

Republic of
NAURU
(central Pacific Ocean)

Bernard **Dowiyogo**, President
Office of the President
NAURU

Kingdom of
NEPAL
(Asia)

HM King **Birendra** Bir Bikram Shah Dev
Narayan Hiti, Royal Palace
Kathmandu
NEPAL

Girija Prasad **Koirala**, Prime Minister
Office of the Prime Minister
Singh Durbar
Kathmandu
NEPAL

Kingdom of
THE NETHERLANDS
(western Europe)

HM Queen **Beatrix** Wilhelmina Armgard
Noordeinde 68
Postbus 30412
2500 GK The Hague
THE NETHERLANDS
Telephone: 70-62-47-01

Dr. Rudolph F.M. **Lubbers**, Prime Minister
Office of the Prime Minister
Binnenhof 20
P.O. Box 20001
2500 EA
The Hague
THE NETHERLANDS
Telephone: (070) 61-40-31

NEW ZEALAND
(southern Pacific Ocean)

Jim **Bolger**, Prime Minister
Office of the Prime Minister
Executive Wing
Parliament Buildings
Wellington
NEW ZEALAND
Telephone: (04) 719998

Republic of
NICARAGUA
(Central America)

Violeta Barrios de **Chamorro**, President
Office of the President
Casa de Gobierno
Managua
NICARAGUA

Republic of
NIGER
(central Africa)

Brig.-Gen. Ali **Saibou**, President and Chairman of the
Supreme Military Council
Office of the President and Chairman
Naimey
NIGER
Telephone: 72-23-81

Aliou **Mahamidou**, Prime Minister
Office of the Prime Minister
Naimey
NIGER

Federal Republic of
NIGERIA
(western Africa)

Gen. Ibrahim **Babangida**, President and Commander-in-Chief of the Armed Forces
Office of the President
State House
Ribadu Road
Ikoyi
Lagos
NIGERIA

Kingdom of
NORWAY
(northern Europe)

HM King **Harald V**
The Royal Palace
Drammensvn. 1
N-0010 Oslo 1
NORWAY
Telephone: (2) 441920

Mrs. Gro Harlem **Brundtland**, Prime Minister
Office of the Prime Minister
Akersgt 42
P.O. Box 8001 Dep.
N-0030 Oslo 1
NORWAY
Telephone: (2) 11-90-90

Sultinate of
OMAN
(southeastern Arabian Peninsula/Gulf of Oman)

QABOOS bin Sa`id Al **Said**, Sultan and Prime Minister
Office of the Sultan and Prime Minister
P.O. Box 252
Muscat
OMAN
Telephone: 699532

Islamic Republic of
PAKISTAN
(southern Asia)

Ghulam **Ishaq Khan**, President
Office of the President
"AWAN-E-SADR"
Mall Road
Mayo Road Crossing
Islamabad
PAKISTAN
Telephone: (51) 820-019

Nawaz **Sharif**, Prime Minister
Office of the Prime Minister
Prime Minister's Secretariat
Old State Bank Building
Islamabad
PAKISTAN

Republic of
PANAMA
(Central America)

Guillermo **Endara**, President
Office of the Commander-in-Chief
Valija 50
Panama'1
PANAMA
Telephone: 22-0520

Independent State of
PAPUA NEW GUINEA
(Pacific Ocean/eastern New Guinea)

Rabbie **Namaliu**, Prime Minister
Office of the Prime Minister
P.O. Box 6605
Boroko
PAPUA NEW GUINEA
Telephone: 277318

Republic of
PARAGUAY
(central South America)

Gen. Andrés **Rodriguez** Pedotti, President
Office of the President
Palacio de Gobierno
Asuncíon
PARAGUAY

Republic of
PERU
(western South America)

Alberto Kenyo **Fujimori** Fujimori, President
Office of the President
Palacio de Gobierno
Plaza de Armas S/N
Lima 1
PERU
Telephone: 271366
FAX: 310427

Carlos Torres y **Torres** Lara, President of Ministeries
Cabinet
Office of the President, Ministries Cabinet
Avda. Abancay 491
Esquina jr Miroquesada
Edificio el Progreso
Piso 8
Lima 1
PERU
Telephone: 270183

Republic of
THE PHILIPPINES
(western Pacific Ocean)

Corazon C. **Aquino**, President
Office of the President
Malacanang Palace Compound
J.P. Laurel Sr. Street
San Miguel, Manila 1005
THE PHILIPPINES
Telephone: (02) 521-2301-10

Republic of
POLAND
(eastern Europe)

Lech **Walesa**, President
Office of the President
Ul. Wiejska 4/8
00-902 Warszawa
POLAND
Telephone: 28-70-01

Jan Krzysztof **Bielecki**, Prime Minister
Office of the Prime Minister
Ul. Wiejska 4/8
00-902 Warszawa
POLAND

PORTUGAL
(western Europe)

Dr. Mário Alberto Nobre Lopes **Soares**, President
Office of the President
Presidência da República
Palácio de Belém
1300 Lisbon
PORTUGAL
Telephone: 637141

Anibal **Cavaco** Silva, Prime Minister
Office of the Prime Minister
Palacio de S. Bento
Lisbon
PORTUGAL
Telephone: 605522

State of
QATAR
(Persian Gulf)

Sheikh Khalifa bin Hamad Al-**Thani**, Amir and Prime
Minister
Technical Office of the Amir
P.O. Box 923
Doha
QATAR
Telephone: 415888

ROMANIA
(southeastern Europe)

Ion **Illiescu**, President
Office of the President
Calea Victoriei 49-53
Bucharest
ROMANIA
Telephone: 14 81 10

(vacant)
Office of the Prime Minister
Str. Academiei 34
Bucharest
ROMANIA
Telephone: 15 02 00

Republic of
RWANDA
(central Africa)

Maj.-Gen. Juvénal **Habyarimana**, President
Office of the President
BP 15
Kigali
RWANDA
Telephone: 5432

Federation of
SAINT KITTS and NEVIS
(West Indies)

Dr. Kennedy Alphonse **Simmonds**, Prime Minister
Office of the Prime Minister
P.O. Box 186
Government Headquarters
Basseterre
SAINT KITTS
Telephone: 809-465-2103
FAX: 809-465-1001

SAINT LUCIA
(West Indies)

John G.M. **Compton**, Prime Minister
Office of the Prime Minister
Castries
SAINT LUCIA
Telephone: 23980

SAINT VINCENT and the GRENADINES

(West Indies)

James F. **Mitchell**, Prime Minister
Office of the Prime Minister
Kingstown
SAINT VINCENT
Telephone: 61703

Republic of SAN MARINO

(southern Europe)

Captains Regent:
Umberto **Barulli** I
Rosolino **Martelli** III
Office of the Captains Regent
San Marino
SAN MARINO

Democratic Republic of
SÃO TOMÉ and PRÍNCIPE
(west central Africa)

Miguel **Trovoada**, President and Commander-in-Chief
of the Armed Forces
Office of the President
São Tomé
SÃO TOMÉ and PRÍNCIPE

Daniel Lima dos Santos **Daid**, Prime Minister
Office of the Prime Minister
São Tomé
SÃO TOMÉ and PRÍNCIPE

Kingdom of
SAUDIA ARABIA
(Persian Gulf)

HM King **FAHD** Bin Abdul Aziz al-Saud
Custodian of the Two Holy Mosques
Royal Court
Riyadh 11111
SAUDIA ARABIA

Republic of
SENEGAL
(western Coast of Africa

Abdou **Diouf**, President
Office of the President
ave. Roume
BP 168
Dakar
SENEGAL
Telephone: 23-10-88

Habib **Thiam**, Prime Minister
Office of the Prime Minister
Dakar
SENEGAL

Republic of
SEYCHELLES
(western Indian Ocean)

France Albert **René**, President
Office of the President
National House
P.O. Box 56
Victoria
SEYCHELLES
Telephone: 24041

Republic of
SIERRA LEONE
(west coast of Africa)

Maj.-Gen. Joseph Saidv **Momoh**, President
Office of the President
Freetown
SIERRA LEONE

Republic of
SINGAPORE
(Southeastern Asia)

Wee Kim Wee, President
Office of the President
Orchard Road
Istana
SINGAPORE 0922
Telephone: 7375522

Goh Chok Tong, Prime Minister
Office of the Prime Minister
Istana Annexe
Istana
SINGAPORE 0923
Telephone: 7375133

SOLOMON ISLANDS
(southwestern Pacific Ocean)

Solomon **Mamaloni**, Prime Minister
Office of the Prime Minister
P.O. Box G1
Honiara
Guadalcanal
SOLOMON ISLANDS
Telephone: 21863

SOMALIA
(eastern Coast of Africa)

Ali Mahdi Mohamed, President
Office of the President
People's Palace
Mogadishu
SOMALIA
Telephone: 723

Omar Artech Ghalib, Prime Minister
Office of the Prime Minister
Mogadishu
SOMALIA

Republic of
SOUTH AFRICA
(southern Africa)

Frederik W. **de Klerk**, State President
Office of the State President
Tuynhuys
Cape Town 8001
SOUTH AFRICA

Kingdom of
SPAIN
(southwestern Europe)

HRH King **Juan Carlos I**, King of Spain, Head of State,
Commander-in-Chief of the Armed Forces, and Head of
Supreme Council of Defense
Palacio de la Zarzuela
Office of the King
Madrid 28071
SPAIN
Telephone: 522-5776
FAX: 532-9543

Felipe **González** Márquez, Prime Minister and President
of the Council
Office of the Prime Minister
Complejo de la Moncloa
Madrid 28071
SPAIN
Telephone: 244-0200

Democratic Socialist Republic of
SRI LANKA
(southern Asia)

Ranasinghe **Premadasa**, President
Office of the President
President's Secretariat
Republic Square
Columbo 1
SRI LANKA
Telephone: (1) 24801
FAX: 941546657

D.B. **Wijetunge**, Prime Minister
Office of the Prime Minister
58 Sir Ernest de Silva Mawatha
Colombo 7
SRI LANKA
Telephone: (1) 433215

Republic of
THE SUDAN
(northeastern Africa)

`Umar Hasan Ahmad al-**Bashir**, Chairman, Revolution-
ary Leadership Council for National Salvation and Prime
Minister
Office of the Chairman and Prime Minister
Khartoum
SUDAN

Republic of
SURINAME
(northeastern Coast of South America)

Johannes Samuel Petrus **Kraag**
Office of the President
Paramaribo
SURINAME

Kingdom of
SWAZILAND
(southern Africa)

HM King **Mswat** III
The King's Office
P.O. Box 1
Lombaba
SWAZILAND
Telephone: 268 61080

Obed Mfanyana **Dlamini**, Prime Minister
Office of the Prime Minister
P.O. Box 395
Mbabane
SWAZILAND
Telephone: 268 42251

Kingdom of
SWEDEN
(northwestern Europe)

King **Carl** XVI Gustaf
Office of the King
The Royal Palace
111 30 Stockholm
SWEDEN

Carl **Bildt**, Prime Minister
Office of the Prime Minister
103 33 Stockholm
SWEDEN
Telephone: (8) 763-10-00

SWITZERLAND
(central Europe)

Flavio **Cotti**, President
Office of the President
Federal Chancellery
Bundeshaus-West
Bundesgasse
3003 Berne
SWITZERLAND
Telephone: (031) 613727

SYRIA
(Middle East)

Gen. Hafiz al-**Assad**, President
Office of the President
Damascus
SYRIA

Mahmud **Zu`bi**, Prime Minister
Office of the Prime Minister
Damascus
SYRIA

United Republic of
TANZANIA
(eastern Coast of Africa)

Ndugu Ali Hassan **Mwinyi**, President
Office of the President
The State House
P.O. Box 9120
Dar es Salaam
TANZANIA
Telephone: 23261

John **Malecela**, Prime Minister
Office of the Prime Minister
Dar es Salaam
TANZANIA

Kingdom of
THAILAND
(southeastern Asia)

HM King **Bhumibol Adulyadej**
Office of the King
Bangkok
THAILAND

Interim Prime Minister: Anand **Panyarachun**
Office of the Prime Minister
Government House
Nakhon Pathom Road
Bangkok 10300
THAILAND

Republic of
TOGO
(western Africa)

Gen. Gnassingbé **Eyadéma**, President
Palais Présidentiel
ave de la Marina
Lome'
TOGO
Telephone: 21-27-01

Kingdom of
TONGA
(southwestern Pacific Ocean)

HM King Taufa'ahau **Tupou** IV
Office of the King
The Palace
Nukúalofa
TONGA

HRH Prince Fatafehi **Tu'ipelehake**, Prime Minister
Office of the Prime Minister
Nukúalofa
TONGA
Telephone: 21305

Republic of
TRINIDAD and TOBAGO
(Caribbean Sea)

Noor **Hassanali**, President
Office of the President
President's House
St. Ann's
TRINIDAD and TOBAGO
Telephone: (809) 624-1261; 7965

Arthur Napoleon Raymond **Robinson**, Prime Minister
Office of the Prime Minister
Central Bank Tower
Eric Williams Plaza
Independence Square South
Port of Spain, Trinidad
TRINIDAD and TOBAGO
Telephone: (809) 623-3653; 3655; 3669

Republic of
TUNISIA
(northern Africa)

Zine El Abidine **Ben Ali**, President
Palais de la Présidence
Carthage
TUNISIA

Dr. Hamed **Karoui**, Prime Minister
Premier Ministère
Place du Gouvernement
La Kasbah, Tunis
TUNISIA

Republic of
TURKEY
(Middle East)

Turgut **Özal**, President
Office of the President
Cumhurbaskanlugu köskü
Cankaya
Ankara
TURKEY

Mesut **Yilmaz**, Prime Minister
Office of the Prime Minister
Basbakanlik
Bakanliklar
Ankara
TURKEY
Telephone: (4) 1186230

TUVALU
(western Pacific Ocean)

Bikenibeu **Paeniu**, Prime Minister
Office of the Prime Minister
Vaiaku
Funafuti
TUVALU

Republic of
UGANDA
(central Africa)

Yoweri Kaguta **Museveni**, President
Office of the President
Parliament Buildings
P.O. Box 7169
Kampala
UGANDA
Telephone: 254881

George Cosmas **Adyebo**, Prime Minister
Office of the Prime Minister
Kampala International Conference Center
P.O. Box 341
Kampala
UGANDA
Telephone: 259758

UNION OF SOVIET SOCIALIST REPUBLICS

(eastern Europe/northern Asia)

Mikhail Sergeyevich **Gorbachev**, President
Office of the Chairman
Staraya pl. 4
Moscow
USSR
Telephone: 206-25-11

SOVIET SOCIALIST REPUBLICS

THE RUSSIAN SOVIET FEDERATIVE SOCIALIST REPUBLIC

Boris N. **Yeltsin**, President
Office of the President
Moscow
USSR

THE ARMENIAN SOVIET SOCIALIST REPUBLIC

S.K. **Tonoyan**, Chairman
Office of the Chairman
Yereuan
ARMENIAN SSR
USSR

THE AZERBAIDZHAN SOVIET SOCIALIST REPUBLIC*

Ayaz Niyaz Ogly **Mutalibov**, Chairman
Office of the Chairman
Baku
AZERBAIDZHAN SSR
USSR

THE BYELORUSSIAN SOVIET SOCIALIST REPUBLIC*

Nikolai Y. **Dementei**, Chairman
Office of the Chairman
Minsk
BYELORUSSIAN SSR
USSR

THE GEORGIAN SOVIET SOCIALIST REPUBLIC*

Zviad K. **Gamsakhurdia**, President
Office of the President
Tbilisi
GEORGIAN SSR
USSR

THE KAZAKH SOVIET SOCIALIST REPUBLIC

Nursultan A. **Nazarbayev**, Chairman
Office of the Chairman
Alma-Ata
KAZAKH SSR
USSR

---

*This republic has declared independence from the Soviet Union.

THE KIRGHIZ SOVIET SOCIALIST REPUBLIC*

Absamat M. **Masaliyeu**, Chairman
Office of the Chairman
Frunze
KIRGHIZ SSR
USSR

THE MOLDAVIAN SOVIET SOCIALIST REPUBLIC*

Mircea **Snegur**, Chairman
Office of the Chairman
Kishinev
MOLDAVIAN SSR
USSR

THE TADZHIK SOVIET SOCIALIST REPUBLIC*

Rakhman **Nabiyeu**, Chairman
Office of the Chairman
Dushanbe
TADZHIK SSR
USSR

THE TURKMEN SOVIET SOCIALIST REPUBLIC

Saparmuryad A. **Niyazov**, Chairman
Office of the Chairman
Ashkabad
TURKMEN SSR
USSR

---

*This republic has declared independence from the Soviet Union.

THE UKRAINIAN SOVIET SOCIALIST REPUBLIC*

Vladimir A. **Ivashko**, Chairman
Office of the Chairman
Kiev
UKRAINIAN SSR
USSR

UZBEK SOVIET SOCIALIST REPUBLIC*

Islam A. **Karlmov**, Chairman
Office of the Chairman
Tashkent
UZBEK SSR
USSR

UNITED ARAB EMIRATES
(Persian Gulf)

Sheikh Zayid bin Sultan Al-**Nuhayyan**, President
Office of the President
Abu Dhabi
UNITED ARAB EMIRATES

Sheikh Maktoum bin Rashid Al-**Maktoum**, Prime Minister
Office of the Prime Minister
P.O. Box 899
Abu Dhabi
UNITED ARAB EMIRATES
Telephone: (2) 361555

---

*This republic has declared independence from the Soviet Union.

UNITED KINGDOM
(northwestern Europe and other locations)

GREAT BRITAIN

HM Queen **Elizabeth** II
Buckingham Palace
SW1
ENGLAND

_____

John **Major**, Prime Minister
Office of the Prime Minister
10 Downing Street
London, SW1A 2AA
ENGLAND
Telephone: (071) 270-3000

_____

NORTHERN IRELAND

Peter **Brooke**, Secretary of State for Northern Ireland
Office of the Secretary of State
Stormont Castle
Belfast, BT4 3ST
NORTHERN IRELAND
Telephone: (0232) 63011/2

UNITED KINGDOM CROWN DEPENDENCIES and DEPENDENT TERRITORIES

ISLE of MAN

M.R. **Walker**, Chief Minister
Office of the Chief Minister
Government House
Douglas
ISLE OF MAN
Telephone: (0624) 26262

ANGUILLA

B.G.J. **Canty**, Governor
Office of the Governor
Government House
The Valley
ANGUILLA
Telephone: (1 809 497) 2622
FAX: (1 809) 497 3151

BERMUDA

Sir Desmond **Langley**, Governor and
Commander-in-Chief
Office of the Governor
Government House
Hamilton
BERMUDA
Telephone: (1 809 29) 2-3600
FAX: (1 809) 29 53823

BRITISH VIRGIN ISLANDS

John Mark Ambrose **Herdman**, Governor
Office of the Governor
Tortola
BRITISH VIRGIN ISLANDS
Telephone:(1 809 49) 2345
FAX:(809) 494-4435

CAYMAN ISLANDS

Alan James **Scott**, Governor
Office of the Governor
Government House BW1
Grand Cayman
CAYMAN ISLANDS
Telephone: (809) 94 97900
FAX: (809) 94 96556

FALKLAND ISLANDS

W.H. **Fullerton**, Governor
Office of the Governor
Port Stanley
FALKLAND ISLANDS
Telephone: 48-2201
FAX: (500) 2212

GIBRALTAR

Admiral Sir Derek **Reffell**, Governor and
Commander-in-Chief
The Convent
BFPO 52
GIBRALTAR
Telephone: (350) 75908
FAX: 76396

HONG KONG

Sir David Clive **Wilson**, Governor
Office of the Governor
Government House
Central
HONG KONG
Telephone: (852) 5-232031 FAX: 010 852 5 8450995

UNITED STATES OF AMERICA
(central North America)

George Herbert Walker **Bush**, President
Office of the President
The White House
1600 Pennsylvania Avenue
Washington, DC 20500
USA
Telephone: (202) 456-1414

Members of Congress
U.S. Senate
Washington, DC 20510
USA

Members of Congress
House of Representatives
Washington, DC 20515
USA

U.S. TERRITORIES

AMERICAN SAMOA

Peter Tale **Coleman**, Governor
Office of the Governor
Pago Pago
AMERICAN SAMOA 96799
Telephone: (684) 633-4116

GUAM

Joseph F. **Ada**, Governor
Office of the Governor
Agaña
GUAM 96910

NORTHERN MARIANA ISLANDS

Pedro T. **Tenorio**, Governor
Office of the Governor
Saipan
NORTHERN MARIANA ISLANDS, MP96950

PUERTO RICO

Rafael **Hernández** Colon, Governor
Office of the Governor
Box 82 Laforteleza
San Juan
PUERTO RICO 00901

U.S. VIRGIN ISLANDS

Alexander A. **Farrelly**, Governor
Office of the Governor
Government House
St. Thomas
U.S. VIRGIN ISLANDS, VI00801
Telephone: (809) 774-0001

Oriental Republic of
URUGUAY
(southeastern Coast of South America)

Luis Alberto **Lacalle**, President
Office of the President
Edif. Libertad
Montevideo
URUGUAY
Telephone: 989310

Republic of
VANUATU
(southwestern Pacific Ocean)

Fred **Timakata**, President
Office of the President
Port Vila
VANUATU

Fr. Walter Hadye **Lini**, Prime Minister
Office of the Prime Minister
P.O. Box 110
Port Vila
VANUATU
Telephone: 2413

State of
THE VATICAN CITY
(within the City of Rome)

His Holiness **Pope John Paul** II
Apostolic Palace
00120 Vatican City
THE VATICAN CITY

Republic of
VENEZUELA
(northern Coast of South America)

Carlos Andrés **Perez**, President
Office of the President
Ave. Urdaneta
Palacio de Miraflores
Caracas
VENEZUELA
Telephone: (582) 810-811

Socialist Republic of
VIETNAM
(southeastern Asia)

Le Quang Dao, Chairman, National Assembly
Office of the Chairman, National Assembly
Hanoi
VIETNAM

Vo Chi Cong, Chairman of the Council of State
Office of the Chairman of the Council of State
Hanoi
VIETNAM

Independent State of
WESTERN SAMOA
(southern Pacific Ocean)

HH Malietoa **Tanumafili** II, O le Ao o Malo
Office of the O le Ao o Malo
Apia
WESTERN SAMOA

Tofilau Eti Alesana, Prime Minister
Office of the Prime Minister
P.O. Box 193
Apia
WESTERN SAMOA
Telephone: 21500

Republic of
YEMEN
(southwestern Arabian Peninsula)

Lt.-Gen. Ali Abdullah **Salih**, President
Office of the President
San`a
YEMEN

Haydar Abu Bakr al-`**Attas**, Prime Minister
Office of the Prime Minister
San`a
YEMEN

Socialist Federal Republic of
YUGOSLAVIA
(southeastern Europe)

Stjepan **Mesic**, President
Office of the President
Palata Federacije
Bul. Lenjina 2
11070 Novi Benograd
YUGOSLAVIA
Telephone: (011) 334-281

Republic of
ZAIRE
(central Africa)

Marshal **Mobutu** Sese Seko Wa Za Banga, President
Office of the President
Mont Ngaliema
Kinshasa
ZAIRE
Telephone: 31312

Lukoji **Mulumba**, Prime Minister
Office of the Prime Minister
Kinshasa
ZAIRE

Republic of
ZAMBIA
(southern central Africa)

Dr. Kenneth David **Kaunda**, President
Office of the President
State House
P.O. Box 30208
Lusaka
ZAMBIA
Telephone: (260-1) 222320

Gen. Malimba N. **Masheke**, Prime Minister
Office of the Prime Minister
P.O. Box 30208
Lusaka
ZAMBIA
Telephone: (260-1) 222409

Republic of
ZIMBABWE
(southern Africa)

Robert Gabriel **Mugabe**, Executive President
Office of the Executive President
P.O. Box 7700, Causeday
Harare
ZIMBABWE
Telephone: 707091

Selected World Organizations and Other Leaders

AFRICAN NATIONAL CONGRESS

Alfred **Nzo**, Secretary General
Office of the Secretary General
African National Congress
P.O. Box 31791
Lusaka
ZAMBIA
Telephone: 1 219656

THE COMMONWEALTH

Sir Shridath S. **Ramphal** (Guyana), Secretary General
The Commonwealth
Commonwealth Secretariat
Marlborough House
Pall Mall
London SW1Y 5HX
ENGLAND
Telephone: (01) 839-3411
FAX: (01) 930 0827

THE DALAI LAMA

The Dalai Lama

Thekehen Choeling
McLeod Ganj 176219
Dharamsala
Himachal Pradesh
INDIA

INTERNATIONAL OLYMPIC COMMITTEE

Francois **Carrard**, General Director
Office of the General Director
International Olympic Committee
Château de Vidy
1007 Lausanne
SWITZERLAND
Telephone: 25.32.71
FAX: 24.15.52

NORTH ATLANTIC TREATY ORGANIZATION (NATO)

Manfred **Wörner**, Secretary General (GE)
Office of the Secretary General
North Atlantic Treaty Organization
1110 Brussels
BELGIUM
Telephone: (02) 728 4917

ORGANIZATION FOR AFRICAN UNITY

Salim Ahmed **Salim**, Secretary General
Office of the Secretary General
Organization for African Unity
P.O. Box 3243
Addis Ababa
ETHIOPIA
Telephone: 517700

ORGANIZATION OF AMERICAN STATES (OAS)

João Clemente Baena **Soares**, Secretary General (Brazil)
Office of the Secretary General
Organization of American States
1889 F Street NW
Washington, DC 20006
USA

ORGANIZATION OF THE PETROLEUM EXPORTING COUNTRIES (OPEC)

HE Dr. **Subroto**, Secretary General
Office of the Secretary General
Organization of Petroleum Exporting Countries
Obere Donaustrasse 93
1020 Vienna
AUSTRIA
Telephone: (0222) 21-11-20
FAX: (0222) 26-43-20

PALESTINE LIBERATION ORGANIZATION

Yasir **Arafat**, Leader
Palestine Liberation Organization
Tunis
TUNISIA

UNITED NATIONS

Javier Pérez de **Cuéllar**, Secretary General
THE UNITED NATIONS
United Nations Building
New York, NY 10017
USA
Telephone: (212) 754-5012

OTHER UNITED NATIONS ADDRESSES:

Palais des Nations
1211 Geneva 10
SWITZERLAND
Telephone: (022) 310211

Vienna International Centre
P.O. Box 500
1400 Vienna
AUSTRIA

OTHER UNITED NATIONS ORGANIZATIONS

LEAGUE OF ARAB STATES
747 3rd Avenue, 35th Floor
New York, NY 10017
Telephone: (212) 838-8700

ORGANIZATION OF AFRICAN UNITY
346 E. 50th Street
New York, NY 10022
Telephone:(212) 319-5490

PALESTINE LIBERATION ORGANIZATION
115 E. 65th Street
New York, NY 10021
(212) 288-8500

WORLD COUNCIL OF CHURCHES

Rev. Dr. Heinz Joachim **Held**, Central Committee
Moderator (FRG)
Office of the Moderator
World Council of Churches
150 route de Ferney
P.O. Box 2100
1211 Geneva 2
SWITZERLAND
Telephone: (022) 7916111
FAX: (022) 7910361

WORLD HEALTH ORGANIZATION

Dr. Hiroshi **Nakajima** (Japan), Director General
Office of the Director General
World Health Organization
Avenue Appia, 1211
Geneva 27
SWITZERLAND
Telephone: (022) 7912111
FAX: (022) 7910746

Leaders and Nations

Ada, Joseph F.; GUAM
Adyebo, George Cosmas; UGANDA
Ahmed, Shahabuddin; BANGLADESH
Aho, Esko; FINLAND
Akihito, HM Emperor; JAPAN
Ali, Mahdi Mohamed; SOMALIA
Alia, Ramiz; ALBANIA
Alingue, Jean Bawoyeu; CHAD
Andreotti, Giulio; ITALY
Antall, József; HUNGARY
Aquino, Corazon C.; THE PHILIPPINES
Arafat, Yasir; PALESTINE LIBERATION ORGANIZATION
Assad, Gen. Hafiz al-; SYRIA
Attas, Haydar Abu Bakr al-; YEMEN
Ausseil, Jean; MONACO
Aylwin, Azocar, Patricio; CHILE
Azlan Muhibbuddin Shah ibni Sultan Yusof Izzudin; MALAYSIA
Babangida, Gen. Ibrahim; NIGERIA

Balaguer Ricardo, Dr. Joaquín; THE DOMINICAN REPUBLIC

Banda, Dr. Hastings Kamuzu; MALAWI

Barkat Gourad Hamadou; DJIBOUTI

Barulli I, Umberto; SAN MARINO

Bashir, `Umar Hasan Ahmad al-; THE SUDAN

Baudouin I, HM King; BELGIUM

Beatrix Wilhelmina Armgard, HM Queen; THE NETHERLANDS

Ben Ali, Zine El Abidine; TUNISIA

Bendjedid Chadli, Col.; ALGERIA

Bhumibol *Adulyadej*, HM King; THAILAND

Bielecki, Jan Krzysztof; POLAND

Bildt, Carl; SWEDEN

Bird, Vere C.; ANTIGUA and BARBUDA

Birendra Bir Bikram Shah Dev, HM King; NEPAL

Bolger, Jim; NEW ZEALAND

Bongo, El Hadj Omar (Albert-Bernard); GABON

Borja Cevallos, Rodrigo; ECUADOR

Brathwaite, Nicholas A.; GRENADA

Brooke, Peter; NORTHERN IRELAND

Brundtland, Mrs. Gro Harlem; NORWAY

Brunhart, Hans; LIECHTENSTEIN

Bufi, Ylli Sokrat; ALBANIA

Bush, George Herbert Walker, UNITED STATES OF AMERICA

Buyoya, Maj. Pierre; BURUNDI

Byambasuren, Dashiyn; MONGOLIA

Calderón Fournier, Rafael Angel; COSTA RICA

Calfa, Marián; CZECHOSLOVAKIA

Callejas, Rafael Leonardo; HONDURAS

Campaoré, Capt. Blaise; BURKINA FASO

Canty, B.G.J.; ANGUILLA
Carl XIV Gustaf, King; SWEDEN
Carrard, Francois; INTERNATIONAL OLYMPIC COMMITTEE
Castro Ruz, Dr. Fidel; CUBA
Cavaco Silva, Anibal; PORTUGAL
Chamorro, Violeta Barrios de; NICARAGUA
Charles, Mary Eugenia; DOMINICA
Chissano, Joaquím Alberto; MOZAMBIQUE
Chung Won-shik; SOUTH KOREA
Coleman, Peter Tale; AMERICAN SAMOA
Collor de Mello, Fernando; BRAZIL
Compton, John G.M.; SAINT LUCIA
Conté, Gen. Lansana; GUINEA
Cotti, Flavio; SWITZERLAND
Cossiga, Francesco; ITALY
Cresson, Edith; FRANCE
Cristiani Buckard, (Felix) Alfredo; EL SALVADOR
Cuéllar, Javier Pérez de; UNITED NATIONS
Daid, Daniel Lima de Santos; SÃO TOMÉ and PRÍNCIPE
Dam, Atli; FAROE ISLANDS
de Klerk, Frederik W.; SOUTH AFRICA
Deby, Idriss; CHAD
Dementei, Nikolai Y.; BEYLORUSSIAN S.S.R.
Diouf, Abdou; SENEGAL
Djohar, Said Mohamed; THE COMOROS
Dlamini, Obed Mfanyana; SWAZILAND
Dorda, Abuzeid Omar; LIBYA
Dowiyogo, Bernard; NAURU
Elizabeth II, HM Queen; UNITED KINGDOM
Emil, Lars; GREENLAND

Endara, Guillermo; PANAMA
Eyadéma, Gen. Gnassingbé; TOGO
Fahd Bin Abdul Aziz al-Saud, HM King
Farrelly, Alexander A.; U.S. VIRGIN ISLANDS
Fenech-Adami, Dr. Edward; MALTA
Finnbogadóttir, Vigdís; ICELAND
Franck, Edouard; CENTRAL AFRICAN REPUBLIC
Fujimori Fujimori, Alberto Kenyo; PERU
Fullerton, W.H.; FALKLAND ISLANDS
Gamsakhurdia, Zviad K.; GEORGIAN SOVIET
SOCIALIST REPUBLIC
Ganilau, Ratu Sir Penaia; FIJI
Gaviria Trujillo; Cesar; COLOMBIA
Gayoom, Maumoon Abdul; MALDIVES
Geingob, Hage; NAMIBIA
Ghozal, Sid Ahmed; ALGERIA
Goh Chok Tong; SINGAPORE
Göncz, Arpád; HUNGARY
González Márquez, Felipe; SPAIN
Gorbachev, Mikhail Sergeyevich; U.S.S.R.
Gorbunous, Anatolijs V.; LATVIA
Grasset, Bernard; FRENCH POLYNESIA
Green Hamilton; GUYANA
Habyarimana, Maj.-Gen. Juvénal; RWANDA
Hammadi, Saadoun; IRAQ
Hans, Adam II; LIECHTENSTEIN
Harald V, HM King; NORWAY
Harawi, Ilyas; LEBANON
Hashemi-Rafsanjani, Ali Akbar; IRAN
Hassan Gouled Aptidon, DJIBOUTI
Hassan II, HM King; MOROCCO

Hassanal Bolkiah Mu'izzaddin Waddaulah, HM Sir Muda Haji; BRUNEI

Hassanali, Noor; TRINIDAD AND TOBAGO

Haughey, Charles J.; IRELAND

Havel, Vaclav; CZECHOSLOVAKIA

Hayatou, P.M. Sadou; CAMEROON

Hawke, Robert J.L.; AUSTRALIA

Held, Rev. Dr. Heinz Joachim; WORLD COUNCIL OF CHURCHES

Herdman, John Mark Ambrose; BRITISH VIRGIN ISLANDS

Hernández, Colon, Rafael; PUERTO RICO

Herzog, Gen. Chaim; ISRAEL

Houphouët-Boigny, Dr. Félix; IVORY COAST

Hoyte, Hugh Desmond; GUYANA

Hun Sen; CAMBODIA

Husayn, Saddam; IRAQ

Hassan II, HM King; MOROCCO

Hussein Ibn Talal, HM King; JORDAN

Illiescu, Ion; ROMANIA

Ishaq Khan, Ghulam; PAKISTAN

Ivashko Vladimir A.; UKRAINIAN S.S.R.

Jawara, Alhaji Sir Dawda Kairaba; THE GAMBIA

Jean, HRH Grand Duke; LUXEMBOURG

Jiang Zemin; PR CHINA

Juan Carlos I, HRH King; SPAIN

Jugnauth, Anerood; MAURITIUS

Kabua, Amata; MARSHALL ISLANDS

Karamanlis, Constantinos; GREECE

Karami, Omar; LEBANON

Karlmov, Islam A.; UZBEK S.S.R.

Karoui, Dr. Hamed; TUNISIA

Kaunda, Dr. Kenneth David; ZAMBIA

Kaysone Phomvihan; LAOS

Khalifa, Sheikh Isa bin Sulman al-; BAHRAIN

Khalifa, Sheikh Khalifa bin Salman al-; BAHRAIN

Khaliqyar, Fazil Haq; AFGHANISTAN

Khamenei, Ali Hoseini-; IRAN

Kim Il-song, Marshal; NORTH KOREA

King, Tom; NORTHERN IRELAND

Kohl, Dr. Helmut; GERMANY

Kolingba, Gen. André-Dieudonne; CENTRAL AFRICAN REPUBLIC

Koirala, Girija Prasad; NEPAL

Koivisto, Dr. Mauno; FINLAND

Kraag, Johannes Samuel; SURINAME

Lacalle, Luis Alberto; URUGUAY

Landsbergis, Vtyautas Z.; LITHUANIA

Langley, Sir Desmond; BERMUDA

Laraki, Dr. Azzedine; MOROCCO

Le Quang Dao; VIETNAM

Lee, Teng-Hui; CHINA (TAIWAN)

Letsie III, HM King; LESOTHO

Li Peng; PR CHINA

Lini, Fr. Walter Hadye; VANUATU

Lubbers, Dr. Rudolph F.M.; THE NETHERLANDS

Machungo, Mário da Graça; MOZAMBIQUE

Mahamidou, Aliou; NIGER

Major, John; GREAT BRITAIN

Maktoum, Sheikh Maktoum bin Rashid Al-; UNITED ARAB EMIRATES

Malecela, John; TANZANIA

Mamaloni, Solomon; SOLOMON ISLANDS

Manley Michael; JAMAICA

Mara, Kamisese; FIJI

Margrethe II, HM Queen; DENMARK

Martelli III, Rosolino; SAN MARINO

Martens, Dr. Wilfried; BELGIUM

Masaliyeu, Absamat M.; KIRGHIZ S.S.R.

Mascarenhas, Antonio Montiero; CAPE VERDE

Masheke, Gen. Malimba N.; ZAMBIA

Masire, Dr. Quett Ketumile Joni; BOTSWANA

Masri, Tahir al-; JORDAN

Meles, Zenawi; ETHIOPIA

Menem, Carlos Saul; ARGENTINA

Mesic, Stjepan; YUGOSLAVIA

Milongo, Andre; THE CONGO

Mitchell, James F.; SAINT VINCENT AND THE GRENADINES

Mitsotakis, Constantinos; GREECE

Mitterrand, François; FRANCE

Miyazawa, Kiichi; JAPAN

Mobutu, Sese Seko Wa Za Banga, Marshal; ZAIRE

Mohamad, Dr. Mahathir bin; MALAYSIA

Moi, Daniel arap; KENYA

Momoh, Maj-Gen. Joseph Saidv; SIERRA LEONE

Montpezat, Jean; FRENCH POLYNESIA

Mswat III, HM King; SWAZILAND

Mubarak, Mohammed Hosni; EGYPT

Mugabe, Robert Gabriel; ZIMBABWE

Mulroney, (Martin) Brian; CANADA

Mulumba, Lukoji; ZAIRE

Museveni, Lt.-Gen. Yoweri Kaguta; UGANDA

Mutalibov, Ayaz Niyaz Ogly; AZERBAIDZHAN S.S.R.

Mwinyi, Ndugu Ali Hassan; TANZANIA
Nabiyeu, Rakhman; TADZHIK S.S.R.
Najibullah, Dr.; AFGHANISTAN
Nakajima, Dr. Hiroshi; WORLD HEALTH
ORGANIZATION
Namaliu, Rabbie; PAPUA NEW GUINEA
Nazarbayev, Nursultan A.; KAZAKH S.S.R.
Nerette, Joseph; HAITI
Niyazov, Saparmuryad A.; TURKMEN S.S.R.
Norodom Sihanouk; CAMBODIA
Nuhayyan, Sheikh Zayid bin Sultan Al-; UNITED ARAB
EMIRATES
Nujoma, Sam; NAMIBIA
Nzo, Alfred; AFRICAN NATIONAL CONGRESS
Obiang Nguema Mbasogo, Brig.-Gen. Teodoro;
EQUATORIAL GUINEA
Ochirbat, Punsalmaagiyn, MONGOLIA
Oddsson, David; ICELAND
Olter, James; MICRONESIA
Omar, Artech Ghalib; SOMALIA
Ouattara, Alassane; IVORY COAST
Oye-Mba, Casimir; GABON
Özal, Turgut; TURKEY
Panyarachun, Anand; THAILAND
Paeniu, Bikenibeu; TUVALU
Paz Zamora, Jaime; BOLIVIA
Perez, Carlos Andrés; VENEZUELA
Pindling, Sir Lynden Oscar; THE BAHAMAS
Pope John Paul II, His Holiness; THE VATICAN CITY
Popov, Dimiter; BULGARIA
Premadasa, Ranasinghe; SRI LANKA

Price, George; BELIZE

Qadhafi, Col. Mu`ammar Abu Minyar al-; LIBYA

Rainier III, HRH Prince; MONACO

Ramahatra, Col. Victor; MADAGASCAR

Ramapma, Col. Elias Phisoana; LESOTHO

Ramphal, Sir Shridath S.; THE COMMONWEALTH

Ratsiraka, Adm. Didier; MADAGASCAR

Rawlings, Flight-Lt. (Ret.) Jerry John; GHANA

Reffell, Admiral Sir Derek; GIBRALTER

René, France Albert; SEYCHELLES

Robinson, Arthur Napoleon Raymond; TRINIDAD AND TOBAGO

Robinson, Mary; IRELAND

Rodriguez Pedotti, Gen. Andrés; PARAGUAY

Roh Tae-Woo; SOUTH KOREA

Rüütel, Arnold F.; ESTONIA

Sabah, HH Sheikh Jabir al-Ahmad al-Jabir Al-; KUWAIT

Sabah, Sheikh Sa`d al-`Abdallah as-Salim Al-; KUWAIT

Saibou, Brig.-Gen. Ali; NIGER

Said, QABOOS bin Sa`id Al; OMAN

Sako, Soumana; MALI

Salih, Lt.-Gen. Ali Abdullah; YEMEN

Salim, Salim Ahmed; ORGANIZATION FOR AFRICAN UNITY

Salinas de Gortari, Carlos; MEXICO

Sandiford, Rt. Hon. Lloyd Erskine; BARBADOS

Santer, Jacques; LUXEMBOURG

Santos, José Eduardo dos; ANGOLA

Sassou-Nguesso, Gen. Denis; THE CONGO

S'Attas, Haydar Abu Bakr al-; YEMEN

Saw Maung, Gen.; BURMA

Sawyer, Amos; LIBERIA
Schlüter, Poul; DENMARK
Scott, Alan James; CAYMAN ISLANDS
Sedky, Dr. Atef; EGYPT
Seignoret, Sir Clarence Augustus; DOMINICA
Serrano Elias, Jorge; GUATEMALA
Shamir, Yitzhak; ISRAEL
Sharif, Nawaz; PAKISTAN
Shezhar, Chandra; INDIA
Sibomana, Adrien; BURUNDI
Simmonds, Dr. Kennedy Alphonse; SAINT KITTS AND NEVIS
Snegur, Mircea; MOLDAVIAN S.S.R.
Soares, Dr. Mário Alberto Nobre Lopes; PORTUGAL
Soares, João Clemente Baena; ORGANIZATION OF AMERICAN STATES
Soeharto, Gen. (Ret.); INDONESIA
Soglo, Nicephore; BENIN
Solans, Josef Pintat; ANDORRA
Souphanouvong; LAOS
Subroto, HE Dr.; OPEC
Tabone, Vincent (Censu); MALTA
Tanumafili II, HH Malietoa; WESTERN SAMOA
Taya, Col. Maaouiya Ould Sid 'Ahmed; MAURITANIA
Taylor, Charles; LIBERIA
Teannaki, Teatao; KIRIBATI
Tenorio, Pedro T.; NORTHERN MARIANA ISLANDS
Thani, Sheikh Khalifa bin Hamad Al-; QATAR
The Dalai Lama
Thiam, Habib; SENEGAL
Timakata, Fred; VANUATU

139

Tofilau Eti Alesana; WESTERN SAMOA

Tonoyan, S.K.; ARMENIAN S.S.R.

Torres Lara, Carlos Torres y; PERU

Toure, Amadou Toumani; MALI

Trovoada, Miguel; SÃO TOMÉ AND PRÍNCIPE

Tu'ipelehake, HRH Prince Fatafehi; TONGA

Tupou IV, HM King Taufa'ahau; TONGA

Vassiliou, George; CYPRUS

Veiga, Carlos Alberto Wahnon de Carvallo; CAPE VERDE

Venkataraman, Ramaswamy Iyer; INDIA

Vieira, Brig.-Gen. Joào Bernardo; GUINEA-BISSAU

Vo Chi Cong, VIETNAM

Vranitzky, Franz; AUSTRIA

Waldheim, Dr. Kurt; AUSTRIA

Walesa, Lech; POLAND

Walker, M.R.; ISLE OF MAN

Wangchuck, HM Jigme Singye; BHUTAN

Wee Kim Wee; SINGAPORE

Weizsäcker, Dr. Richard von; GERMANY

Wijetunge, D.B.; SRI LANKA

Wilson, Sir David Clive; HONG KONG

Wörner, Manfred; NORTH ATLANTIC TREATY ORGANIZATION

Yang Shangkun; PR CHINA

Yeltsin, Boris N.; RUSSIAN S.F.S.R.

Yilmaz, Mesut; TURKEY

Yon Hyong-muk; NORTH KOREA

Zhelev, Zhelyu; BULGARIA

ZIAur Rahman, Khaleda; BANGLADESH

Zu`bi, Mahmud; SYRIA

References

The following books and materials were utilized in the preparation of this book. Many of these books are available at your local library at the reference desk.

Chiefs of State and Cabinet Members of Foreign Governments, published Feb., April, June, Aug., Oct. and Dec. by Central Intelligence Agency, U.S. Government (edition used, Aug. 1991).

Europa Year Book, 1990, A World Survey, Volumes I and II, Europa Publications Limited, London, England, 1990.

Foreign Consular Offices in the United States, Department of State Publication 7846, 1990.

The Statesman's Handbook 1990–91, Edited by John Paxton, MacMillan Press, LTD, London, England, 1991.

Who's Who 1989, A&C Black, London, England, 1989.

There may be additional references useful to you; ask your reference librarian.

About the Author

Rick Lawler is an avid letter-writer, has been all his life. This week he's already fired off letters to the police chief of the city where he lives, to the president of a national company, and to the letters page of the local newspaper. He received a reply to a letter he'd recently written to his congressman.

The author of *How to Write to World Leaders* met his wife through the mails in a long-distance relationship between California and Taiwan. Almost a year after that first, halting written communication, Rick flew to Taiwan and he and Alice Tang were married. Alice joined him in California a few months later—and that was 10 years ago.

Lawler, a former newspaper editor, is currently a freelance writer. His articles have appeared in *Westways, Young World, General Aviation News, Sales and Marketing Management, The Business Journal*, and others. His fiction has been published in *Pulphouse, Mature Years, Space and Time, Ellipsis . . . , Gas*, and others. Rick is employed by the University of California, Davis Medical Center in Sacramento, California and lives in Sacramento with his wife, and their daughter.

He is a member of the Authors Guild and National Writers Club.

He is working on several other book manuscripts, including *MYTH: The Extinction Factor* and a novel, *The Last Barbarian*. He is completing research on a scholarly work, *The History of the Ku Klux Klan in California, 1922*. In 1990, Blair Publications published *Valley Fire*, excerpts from Lawler's experiences as a newspaper reporter in the southcentral California area.

He has won several awards as an amateur photographer, and he collects historic newspapers as a hobby.

He believes in the power of the written word and in the power of public opinion.

For information on updates, write to:
MinRef Press, 8379 Langtree Way,
Sacramento, California 95823